JUN 2011

Ripley's Believe It or Not!

Developed and produced by Ripley Publishing Ltd

This edition published and distributed by:
Mason Crest Publishers Inc.
370 Reed Road, Broomall, Pennsylvania 19008
(866) MCP-BOOK (toll free)
www.masoncrest.com

Ripley's Believe it or Not!
Fantastic Feats
ISBN 978-1-4222-2019-1 (hardcover)
ISBN 978-1-4222-2053-5 (paperback)

Library of Congress Cataloging-in-Publication data is available

Ripley's Believe it or Not!—Complete 16 Title Series
ISBN 978-1-4222-2014-6

1st printing
10 9 8 7 6 5 4 3 2 1

Library of Congress Cataloging-in-Publication Data is available.
Printed in USA

PUBLISHER'S NOTE
While every effort has been made to verify the accuracy of the entries in this book, the
Publisher's cannot be held responsible for any errors contained in the work. They would
be glad to receive any information from readers.

WARNING
Some of the stunts and activities in this book are undertaken by experts and should not
be attempted by anyone without adequate training and supervision.

The Remarkable... Revealed

Mason Crest Publishers

FANTASTIC FEATS

Outstanding achievements. You'll be stunned at

how far people will push their bodies and minds

when you read this book. Find out about the

strongman who breaks metal bars on his head, the

sword swallower who swallows blades up to

24 in (61 cm) long, and the snake charmer who

kissed a venomous snake 51 times in three minutes.

Roderick Russell makes a living by inserting
deadly blades into his esophagus...

SET IN CONCRETE

In memory of his hero, Harry Houdini, Canadian escape artist Dean Gunnarson freed himself from a locked Plexiglas box filled with two tons of wet cement. He was the first person in the world to attempt such a great escape. Not even Houdini himself had tried it.

The sensational stunt, was timed to take place in Winnipeg at 1.26 p.m. on Halloween 2006 (the exact 80th anniversary of Houdini's death). Gunnarson was bound with several pairs of police handcuffs that were chained and padlocked around his waist and entire body, and tightly around his neck. He was then lowered into the box, the cement was poured in, and the lid of the box was locked tight with six maximum-security padlocks so that he was totally encased in a concrete prison.

To the amazement of the crowd, who could see his every move, Gunnarson escaped from his would-be tomb in 2 minutes 43 seconds. He had to get out before being crushed and suffocated by the sheer weight of the cement. "It felt like being crushed by a boa constrictor," said Gunnarson, who had trained for the death-defying ordeal by wriggling in fast-setting cement. "I could feel it pushing against my ribs and lungs every time I struggled." But he emerged with nothing worse than cement burns.

His inspiration for the stunt came when he escaped while dangling by his toes from a trapeze bar while locked in a straightjacket, 726 ft (221 m) above the Hoover Dam just outside Las Vegas. He learned that some workers had been killed while working on the dam, having been buried alive after falling into wet cement. "I thought to myself, 'What a horrible way to go.'"

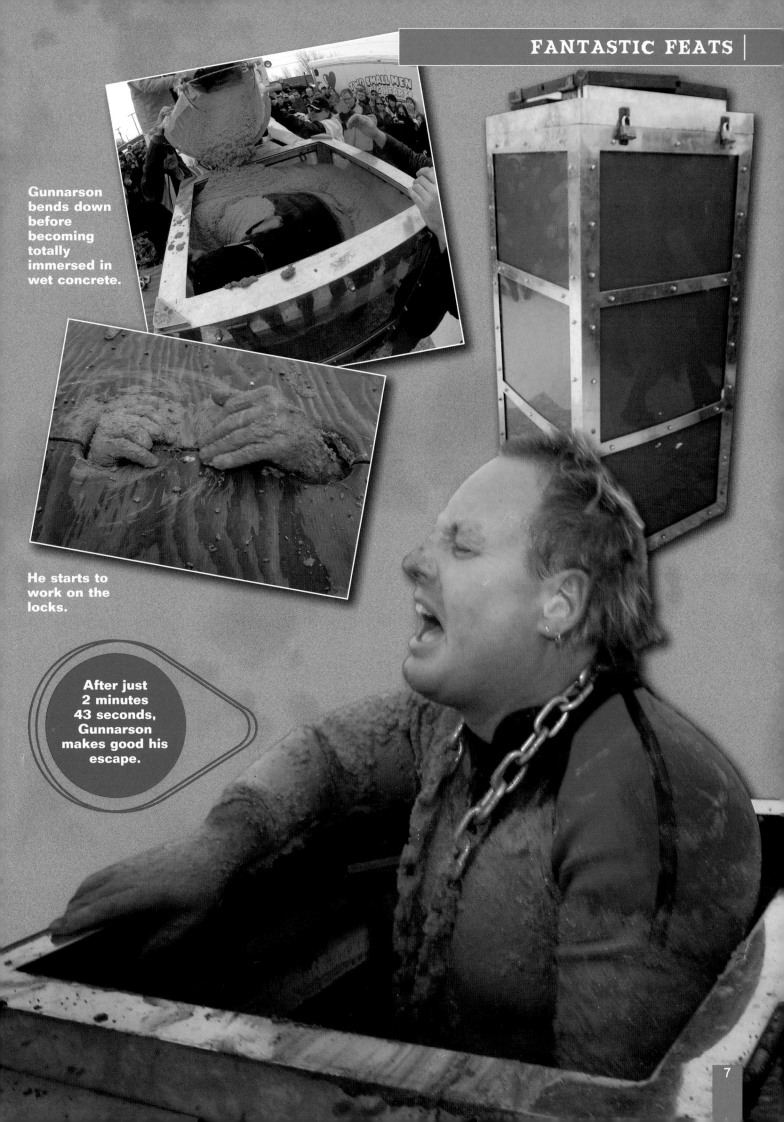

Gunnarson bends down before becoming totally immersed in wet concrete.

He starts to work on the locks.

After just 2 minutes 43 seconds, Gunnarson makes good his escape.

ALCATRAZ SWIM

Fueled by pizza, seven-year-old Braxton Bilbrey of Glendale, Arizona, swam the notoriously difficult 1.4 mi (2 km) from Alcatraz Island to San Francisco in just 47 minutes in 2006.

COMBINE SPEED

In August 2006, 105 combines harvested a quarter section of winter wheat (160 acres/65 ha) near Winkler, Manitoba, Canada, in just 11 minutes 8 seconds.

BIG BUFFET

Diners had an overwhelming choice of food at the Las Vegas Hilton, Nevada, in March 2006 when a buffet was laid out featuring no fewer than 510 different dishes. They ranged from Mongolian chicken and salmon Wellington to crème brûlée and homemade apple pie.

HUGGING SAINT

Mata Amritanandamayi, an Indian humanitarian known as "The Hugging Saint," travels around the world giving hugs—she has given an estimated 26 million hugs during the past 35 years!

SILVER BALL

Stanley Jollymore of Brule Point, Nova Scotia, has spent the last 20 years creating a 77-lb (35-kg) silver ball made from over 139,000 tinfoil cigarette wrappers.

SPOON ENSEMBLE

A street-theater group rounded up 345 spoon players to bash out pub favorite "Knees Up Mother Brown" in Trowbridge, Wiltshire, England, in 2006. The spoons are played by holding two spoons between the fingers of one hand with the bowls facing each other and tapping them against a leg.

△ GIANT'S STRENGTH

Eddie Polo, known to all as "Little Giant," drew quite a crowd when he managed to pull this car 100 yd (91 m) along the road in Dover, New Hampshire, in 1937—using only his hair.

BACKWARDS RUNNER

A Brazilian pensioner claimed he owes his health to his unusual fitness regime of running 19 mi (31 km) every day—backward. Ary Brasil, 69, from Joacaba, has been running since he was 16 but started going backward only six years ago. "I used to feel a lot of pain in my back and legs," he said, "but I found that by running backward I felt less out of breath and my muscles got stronger. It's been nine years since I had a cold and I don't even remember the last time I went to the doctor."

GROUCHO GATHERING

The town of Gorham, Maine, achieved an unusual claim to fame in July 2006 when nearly 1,500 people gathered together wearing Groucho Marx disguises! A total of 1,489 residents turned out wearing the familiar glasses, oversized nose, bushy eyebrows, and mustache.

QUICK CARVER

Stephen Clarke of Haverton, Pennsylvania, can carve a face into a pumpkin in less than 25 seconds!

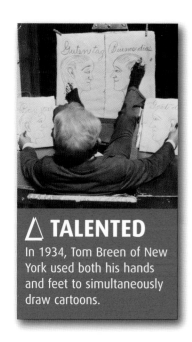

△ TALENTED

In 1934, Tom Breen of New York used both his hands and feet to simultaneously draw cartoons.

BARKING BIKERS

At the 2006 Hogs for Dogs charity run at Amherst, New York, Harley-Davidson bikers brought their dogs along for the ride. Some pets sat on the passenger seat, but Beau, Don Wereski's Maltese Yorkshire, rode in a carrier across his chest. "He goes everywhere with me," said Wereski. "He loves the ride."

VAST VERSE

In 2006, a Frenchman produced a poem of epic proportions—nearly 7,600 verses written on a half-mile roll of fabric. Patrick Huet spent a month and a half composing "Pieces of Hope to the Echo of the World" and then a further month copying it on to the material, which was unrolled with the help of a tractor and put on display around a racetrack in southeast France.

HENDRIX TRIBUTE

In May 2006, 1,581 guitarists simultaneously played Jimi Hendrix's "Hey Joe" at the Old Town Square in Wrocław, Poland. The guitarists traveled from Germany, Hungary, the Netherlands, Sweden, and even the U.S.A. to take part.

FAIRWAY TO HEAVEN

Don't tell Tiger Woods, but a Russian man has driven a golf ball over a billion miles! In 2006, cosmonaut Mikhail Tyurin launched the ball into orbit using a gold-plated six iron from a special tee attached to a platform on the International Space Station 220 mi (355 km) above Earth. Scientists say the ball is likely to circle the Earth for up to four years at a speed of five miles per second before falling from orbit and burning up in the atmosphere.

BICYCLE BELLS

Conducted by Jörg Kärger, 500 people played six pieces of music on bicycle bells at the University of Leipzig, Germany, in 2003.

FURMAN'S FEATS

Ashrita Furman, a 52-year-old health-food store manager from New York City, shows no sign of easing up. The man who has climbed Mount Fuji on a pogo stick, somersaulted the entire length of Paul Revere's ride, and ran 7 mi (11 km) in Egypt while balancing a pool cue on his finger didn't stop there. Among other achievements, he balanced on a ball at Stonehenge, England, for more than two hours, did 9,628 sit-ups in an hour, and ran 6 mi (10 km) in 1 hour 25 minutes while hula hooping!

EYES AND EARS

Zhang Yingmin from China's Shandong Province, seen here in 2006, has an unusual method of inflating balloons—he blows them up by expelling air from his eyes and ears!

HOOP ENTHUSIAST

Ohio-born mother-of-three Lori Lynn Lomeli is never happier than when surrounded by hula hoops. Introduced to hula hooping at the age of eight, she once made headlines for spinning 82 hoops simultaneously for three complete revolutions in Reno, Nevada.

LITTLE ▷ DRUMMER

Two-year-old American Julian Pavone has already played the drums in front of 30,000 people! According to his father, Bernie, Julian started playing a drum set at just three months. He has even made his own CD.

MILK MACHINE

Joey Chestnut of San José, California, drank a gallon of milk in 41 seconds to qualify for the 2006 Philadelphia Wing Bowl eating contest, and then ate 173 chicken wings to win the competition!

RADIO REV

Jay and Jason Plugge of Sunnyvale, California, have invented a car radio that plays the engine sounds of classic cars and motorbikes, including Ferraris, Corvettes, and Harley-Davidsons from the 1950s, 1960s, and 1970s.

STRETCH SARI

Weavers in India created a silk sari that is 1,585 ft (483 m) long and more than 4 ft (1.2 m) wide. Up to 120 weavers worked 24 hours a day on it for more than 80 days, and the finished article weighed over 125 lbs (57 kg).

TEMPORARY PARK

In November 2005, the arts group Rebar transformed a downtown San Francisco parking space into a temporary park. They put coins in the meter and proceeded to position turf, a bench, and a tree to create a green space for two hours. In a previous venture, they spent five days digging a filing cabinet into the New Mexico desert to serve as a library.

INSECT FEAST

To mark Montreal Insectarium's 15th birthday in 2005, the attraction staged an insect-tasting celebration—a six-legged lunch prepared by chef Nicole-Anne Gagnon. The menu included atta ants in a tortilla, roasted crickets served on a cucumber canapé, barbecued locusts, and bruschetta with olive tapenade and bamboo worms.

DOGGIE SURFING

The world's first canine surfing championships took place in California in 2006 at, naturally enough, the Coronado Dog Beach. Riding the waves on custom-made dog surfboards, each surf-loving hound had three chances to impress a panel of professional surfing instructors. The animals were scored on confidence level, length of ride, and overall surfing abilities.

◁ NEWSPAPER MODELS

Zhu Zhonghe from Shanghai, China, at the age of 70, discovered the art of making models created entirely from newspaper. He has made the Eiffel Tower, a Dutch windmill, bridges, boats, and the former residence of the late Chairman Mao Zedong.

SWORD SWALLOWER

Roderick Russell makes a living by inserting blades 24 in (61 cm) long into his esophagus. The average adult esophagus ranges in length from 12 to 15 in (30 to 38 cm), so the Burlington, Vermont, sword swallower, gambles with death every time he performs his routine.

Russell learned the art of sword swallowing in Italy and practiced three times a day for a year before he was ready to perform in front of an audience. The first thing he had to master was the gag reflex. Some swallowers perfect this with an unbent wire coat hanger or a peacock feather, but Russell used a sword from the outset. He also learned that the esophagus isn't as straight as a sword.

"The stomach is much shallower than it appears," he says, "and it curves to the left. The epiglottis and trachea were surprisingly difficult obstacles for me to push past. I learned to push the epiglottis closed with my hand before learning to control it with the tip of a sword. Then I hold my breath for a split second as the sword glides past the closed epiglottis. Getting past the heart is always a touchy moment. I need to turn the sword a little to the left to get into my stomach."

Russell took up sword swallowing to help audiences realize they could achieve anything they wanted. He describes the art as the Holy Grail of mind over body techniques. So far, the mind is definitely winning, although he does take one precaution. "Before I swallow a sword, I always lick the blade. A dry sword is even more difficult to swallow."

X rays show just how far down Russell has actually swallowed a sword.

ROOFTOP MUSIC

In 2006, three "extreme cellists"—Clare Wallace, Jeremy Dawson and James Rees—set out to play on the roof of every cathedral in England! They visited all 42 Anglican cathedrals in England over 12 days, and were allowed to play on the roofs of 31 of them. Their repertoire included "Up on the Roof" and "Climb Every Mountain."

AIR GUITARIST

After years of mocking air guitarists, Craig Billmeier of Alameda, California, finally realized that they struck a chord with him. And four months and two victories after entering a regional competition, Billmeier (whose stage name is "Hot Lixx Hulahan") was crowned U.S. Air Guitar Champion of 2006. Contestants at air guitar competitions play for 60 seconds while judges mark them on technical ability and stage presence.

△ TWO-HANDED BOWLER

Edward Soloff from Atlantic City, New Jersey, was able to bowl two games in two different bowling lanes simultaneously in 1930. What's more, he averaged an impressive score of 270 points for each of the games.

BAND OF OUTLAWS

A total of 307 children, dressed as legendary British outlaw Robin Hood, gathered at Ravenshead Church of England Primary School in Sherwood Forest, Nottinghamshire, England, in March 2006. The children provided their own outfits, including bows and arrows, and made their green hats in school.

HOGWARTS MODEL

Pat Acton of Gladbrook, Iowa, has created detailed and realistic models of ships, airplanes, space shuttles, and buildings—all from matchsticks. His first project 30 years ago was a country church that took 500 matchsticks and a couple of days to complete. His latest, a model of the Hogwarts School immortalized in J.K. Rowling's *Harry Potter* books, took more than two years and 600,000 matchsticks!

SUPER SMOOTHIE

After 3½ hours of blending, using seven blenders, a store in Kitchener, Ontario, Canada, produced a 25,000-oz (740-l) smoothie in August 2006. The monster drink was sold afterwards in 24-oz cups.

SKETCH SKILL

A group of around 3,000 people collaborated in drawing a giant teapot on a huge Etch A Sketch™ that measured 20 x 35 ft (6 x 11 m) at Boston, Massachusetts, in 2006.

LENGTHY LECTURE

Botany lecturer Anniah Ramesh of Mysore, India, delivered a talk on "Molecular Logic of Life" in March 2006 that lasted for over 98 hours! He spoke continuously for three days and three nights until aching legs and sleepless nights finally took their toll. He was so tired that he could be seen dozing while writing on the blackboard.

ROLLER RIDERS

Marriage is definitely a roller coaster ride for Don Tuttle and Carol Deeble. The couple from Manchester, Connecticut, were married on their favorite roller coaster, the Comet at Lake George, New York, in 2001, and in 2006 they renewed their vows on it. In all they have ridden nearly 750 roller coasters in 15 countries, and visited Japan in 2005 and South Africa in 2006 to add to their list.

VENDING FUN △

On October 21, 2006, Robert Moore, aged 3, unhappy at his unsuccessful attempts at scooping out a stuffed toy with the machine's plastic crane, decided to go in and get one. He climbed into the stuffed animal vending machine at a small store in Antigo, Wisconsin. Robert was later rescued by the Antigo Fire Department, who broke the lock and passed a screwdriver to Robert, who managed to undo the necessary screws to effect his release!

MODEL REBUILT

A detailed plastic model of Australia's Sydney Opera House, which had taken seven years to make but had vanished after appearing at the Washington World Expo in 1974, was painstakingly reassembled in 2006 after being found inside 24 storage crates at a Sydney warehouse. With no drawings or plans for guidance, it took 2,000 hours to rebuild the model, the exercise being described as being "like a giant jigsaw."

BALLOON EXPERT

As a boy, Nate Mikulich was fascinated by magic and when, at the age of 13, he met balloon artist Crazy Richard, he became hooked on making animals from balloons. These days, Mikulich of Eastern Michigan is so skilled at the art that he can tie a balloon poodle behind his back in under eight seconds.

WEIGHTY BALLS

In Germany in 2006, Milan Roskopf from Slovakia juggled three shot balls weighing a hefty 22 lb (10 kg) each for 15.8 seconds. He started to juggle balls at the age of nine, moving from small balls to cricket balls, to 2.2 lb (1 kg) balls cast in bronze.

BiG BAND BALL

This giant rubber-band ball was made from more than 175,000 rubber bands in November 2006. Seen here being rolled toward a set of scales, it weighed an incredible 4,594 lb (2,084 kg). It was created by Steve Milton from Eugene, Oregon, who spent a few minutes a day, for just over a year, adding bands to his ball. The result reaches 5½ ft (1.7 m) in height, and has a circumference of 19 ft (5.8 m).

OUTSIZE PAINTING

Working for two and a half years and using 100 tons of paint, artist David Aberg produced a painting that measured a staggering 86,000 sq ft (7,990 sq m). The picture, titled "Mother Earth," is a symbol for peace and is so big it had to be created inside an aircraft hangar in Angelholm, southern Sweden.

TRICKY TEXTER

Tell Ben Cook he's all thumbs and he'll probably take it as a compliment. For the 18-year-old from Orem, Utah, proved himself an expert texter in July 2006, by sending a 160-character message in just over 42 seconds at a contest in Denver, Colorado.

BALLOON FEAT

John Cassidy of Philadelphia, Pennsylvania, inflated and tied more than 700 balloons in an hour at New York City in May 2006. Cassidy has also completed 654 balloon sculptures in an hour.

ATV PARADE

Members of Harlan County, Kentucky, ATV club paraded over 1,100 all-terrain vehicles one Saturday in 2006. The parade began in Verda and ended 2 mi (3.2 km) away in Evarts.

TALL STORY

Canadian stilt walker Doug Hunt has taken 29 independent steps on a pair of stilts 50 ft 9 in (15.5 m) tall and weighing a combined 137 lb (62 kg).

PILLOW FIGHT

Nearly 1,000 people lured by Internet postings and word-of-mouth took part in a half-hour outdoor pillow fight in San Francisco on Valentine's Day 2006. Participants arrived with pillows concealed in shopping bags, backsacks, and the like, and within minutes the area around the city's Ferry Building was covered in white down.

DUAL TALENT

Drew Tretick, a graduate of the prestigious Juilliard School of Music in New York City, who now lives in southern California, plays beautiful tunes on the violin—while riding a unicycle!

BUMPER BEACH TOWEL

A gigantic terry-cloth beach towel was unveiled at Hermosa Beach, California, in June 2006. It measured 131 x 78 ft (40 x 24 m) and weighed nearly 1,000 lb (454 kg).

QUICK CLEANER

If you want your windows cleaned quickly, ask Terry Burrows. At Birmingham, England, in 2005, Burrows cleaned three windows, each measuring 45 in (114 cm) square, and wiped the sill—all in under 10 seconds!

GUITAR SOLO

Apart from a short break every eight hours, Chicago musician Jef Sarver played the guitar uninterrupted for 48 hours in 2006. Sarver, who prepared for the challenge by doing push-ups and sit-ups, played a set of more than 600 songs.

FOIL ART

Pete Schwickrath from Piscataway, New Jersey, makes sculptures from household tin foil, which he then paints. Here, a newly transformed werewolf threatens a young maiden.

SNAKE KISSER

Malaysian snake charmer Shahimi Abdul Hamid kissed a wild, venomous king cobra 51 times in three minutes outside Kuala Lumpur in March 2006. He used agility, skill, and quick reflexes to dodge bites from the 15-ft (4.6-m) snake with only his bare hands to protect him. He was also an hour's drive from the nearest hospital—a daunting prospect considering that a person can be killed with just one drop of cobra venom, and each bite can produce up to 12 drops of poison.

STRAW CHAIN

Brad Mottashed, Evgueni Venkov, and 18 fellow students of Waterloo University, Ontario, Canada, made a straw chain 28,158 ft (8,580 m) long in April 2006 using 50,000 drinking straws.

SNOWBALL FIGHT

More than 3,700 people took part in a mass snowball fight at Houghton, Michigan, in February 2006!

EYELID FEAT

In 2005, Chinese Yang Guanghe fitted hooks to his eyelids and proceeded to pull a car along a street!

MUTTON BUSTIN'

At just eight years old, Ryan Murphy was already a retired champion. Ryan's chosen sport was riding sheep rodeo-style, or "mutton bustin'" as it is popularly known. At the 2006 Truckee Rodeo at Sierra, Nevada, Ryan won the title for the second successive year but has now retired because he has exceeded the riding weight limit of 60 lb (27 kg). The secret of his success was to sit on the sheep backward so as to get a better grip. Whereas other riders quickly bit the dust, Ryan's individual style helped him to stay on for an unbeatable 22 seconds.

KICK LINE

Over 700 people put their best foot skyward at the Algonquin Arts Plaza parking lot, Manasquan, New Jersey, in August 2006 to form a kick line. As well as dance students, the long line included men in sneakers, women in sandals, and teenage boys in surfer shorts and flip-flops.

FOOTPRINT TRAIL

National Geographic Kids magazine spent 1½ days taping together 10,932 paper footprints that zigzagged 1.8 mi (2.9 km) heel-to-toe along the walls and hallways of its headquarters in Washington, D.C. The footprints had been submitted by children from as far away as Australia, Japan, and Mongolia. One was from a child with six toes!

HUMAN FLAG

In May 2006, over 18,000 people gathered in Lisbon's soccer stadium to create a human depiction of the Portuguese national flag.

KAZOO PARADE

In 2006, more than 500 people turned out on the streets of Nazareth, New Jersey, to celebrate the Fourth of July by playing the kazoo.

OLD PRICES

Michael "Mickey" Di Fater of Greenburgh, New York, celebrated his 75th year selling hot dogs by rolling back his prices to 10 cents for a hot dog and a nickel for a soda!

MELON GROWER

Ivan Bright of Hope, Arkansas, devoted the last 30 years of his life to raising huge watermelons, notably a 268-lb (122-kg) Carolina Cross. He died at the age of 92 on August 12, 2006—the 30th anniversary of the Hope Watermelon Festival.

WATER-SKI CHALLENGE

Dirk Gion went water-skiing behind a huge German cruise liner in 2006 to disprove a claim made on TV that the feat was impossible. The 40-year-old stayed upright for more than five minutes.

PENGUIN AIRLIFT

After more than 100 penguins were left stranded on beaches in Rio de Janeiro, Brazil, in 2006, the Brazilian air force and navy transported them safely back to Antarctica. Penguins arrive from the Antarctic on ice floes that melt near Brazil's coast every winter and the flightless birds then find themselves washed up on Rio's beaches. Usually they are sent to local zoos but this time the military intervened.

A REAL MOUTHFUL

In 2006, the city of Nanjing, in eastern China, played host to a TV show that featured people with highly unusual skills. Zhang Dong, shown here inserting a huge spoon into his mouth, was one of the show's participants.

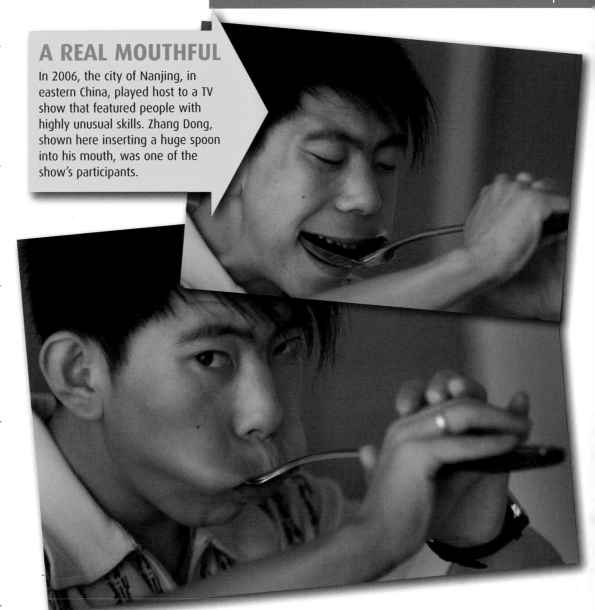

TRUCK DRINK

Rather than drink Milo (a milk beverage with chocolate) from a glass, 620 staff and students at the National University of Singapore decided to drink it from the back of a truck! They drank 92 gal (350 l) of Milo from the truck in 30 minutes.

BABY MARATHON

The city of Cali in Colombia hosted a crawling marathon for babies in 2006—and more than 1,100 babies took part. Infants aged between 8 and 18 months were eligible and they crawled along a 16-ft (5-m) covered track. The winner's prize was a bag full of baby goodies.

ELVIS PARADE

In a variety of sequined jumpsuits, bright pink jackets, and blue suede shoes, 94 sideburned, hip-swivelling Elvises took to the stage at Collingwood, Ontario, Canada, in July 2006 to perform the King's classic hit "All Shook Up."

MASSIVE MURAL

In 2006, Boeing completed a mural on its factory building in Everett, Washington, that takes up more than 100,000 sq ft (9,290 sq m) of pressure-sensitive graphic film. It consists of some 475 sheets, each 60 x 4 ft (18 x 1.2 m) and took over five months to install.

BOWLING MISSION

Larry Woydziak from Lawrence, Kansas, made it his mission to bowl in every county in Kansas that had a bowling alley. He bowled his 79th and final game in the town of Sterling.

BRA CHAIN

Hundreds of volunteers linked together more than 114,700 bras around Paphos harbor in west Cyprus in April 2006 to form a 70-mi (113-km) long chain to raise breast-cancer awareness. Bras were flown to Cyprus from all over the world, including Canada, the U.S.A., Thailand, Brazil, Russia, Iran, and all 25 European Union member states.

BOARD SURFER

A French veterinary surgeon became the first person to cross the shark-infested Indian Ocean on a sailboard.

Raphaela Le Gouvello of Brittany, France, landed on the island of Réunion, off the eastern coast of Africa, in June 2006, having completed a solo 3,900-mi (6,300-km) voyage from Exmouth in Western Australia. Throughout much of the 60-day journey she battled seasickness, strong winds, and rough seas. She made the epic crossing on a simple board—26 ft (8 m) long and 4 ft (1.2 m) wide—named Mahi Mahi. Her board capsized twice, and on one occasion cost her essential supplies of fresh water. Mme Le Gouvello said that although the heavy winds had been a problem, the hardest times were when there was no wind at all. "I couldn't make any progress," she said. "I waited below deck, being tossed around in all directions. It wasn't very comfortable."

When not steering on her eight-hour shifts, she kept herself occupied by listening to music and reading books. She did not fish in case she attracted sharks. Before the trip, she overcame her fear of sharks by diving with them in an aquarium in France.

www.raphaela-legouvello.com

The tiny cabin— just 2 ft 6 in (76 cm) high— housed a bed, spare sails, food, and communication equipment.

Raphaela is no stranger to solo sailboard voyages. She was the first woman to cross the Atlantic and the Mediterranean on a sailboard, and in 2003 she became the first person to cross the Pacific by board.

Raphaela tests her board off Fremantle in Western Australia before setting off on her epic voyage.

SIMULTANEOUS CARTWHEELS

Almost 1,000 people, wearing an array of leotards, T-shirts, and shorts, converged on the Minnesota State Capitol lawn at St. Paul in 2006 to perform an amazing display of simultaneous cartwheels.

SPEEDY HAIRDRESSER

Even at the age of 71, Trevor Mitchell can give a decent haircut in less than a minute. To prove it, in August 2006 he clipped exactly 1 in (2.5 cm) of hair from all over the head of former England soccer manager Kevin Keegan in just 59 seconds.

JONES GATHERING

A small town in North Wales united 1,224 people with the same surname in November 2006. Blaenau Ffestiniog out-performed Sweden, which had previously held an assembly of 583 Norbergs, by inviting anyone around the world with the surname Jones to a 1,600-seater venue. The town was chosen for the gathering because the area boasts the highest concentration of Joneses in Britain.

POLISHED ▷ PICTURES

Mary Scott from Horn Lake, Mississippi, is an artist with a difference—she paints using bottles of nail polish. Mary has a collection of more than 1,000 colors, and uses as many as 30 bottles of polish to create one painting. She paints with the small brushes that come with the bottles and has to work rapidly, because the polish dries very quickly.

SKYDIVING DOG

Wearing a specially made harness and a diaper—in case of mid-air accidents—Mindy, a three-year-old Jack Russell terrier, went skydiving in 2006 with the Jonoke Skydive Team in Alberta, Canada. Diving under a canopy strapped to a tandem skydiving master, Mindy made a successful free-fall of 9,000 ft (2,743 m) in 40 seconds. Her owner, Al Christou, said: "She kept looking at us on the way down. When she landed the first time, she was spinning around in circles."

REVERSE SPELLER

Eight-year-old Raghav Srivathsav from Hyderabad, India, has made a name for himself by spelling words backward. He first started doing this aged three and can now spell 50 words in reverse in under three minutes, and can reverse spell any word or line given to him in just a few seconds.

WATERY CONFERENCE

Wearing full diving gear, a group of 21 Austrian journalists swam 16 ft (5 m) below the surface of the Traun Lake to stage an underwater press conference in June 2006! An underwater flipchart was set up for the presentation and the reporters were given special waterproof paper and pens to enable them to take notes.

NUMERICAL GENIUS

If you give Nishant Kasibhatia a number, he's unlikely to forget it—for 10 years! The 33-year-old Indian man has a phenomenal memory for numbers, having started at the age of 17 by memorizing 100-digit numbers before graduating to 1,000 digits. He can now recite 1,000-digit numbers in reverse order and in 2005 he memorized 200 binary numbers in just over three minutes and recalled them in five minutes without a single mistake.

PIZZA ORDER

Papa John's delivered an order of 13,500 pizzas to San Diego's NASSCO Shipyard on June 8, 2006. To meet the 11 a.m. delivery time, Papa John's used the resources of 15 San Diego restaurants, beginning at 6 a.m., with each making around 56 pizzas per minute throughout the morning—that's nearly one pizza per second! The 2,725 lbs (1,236 kg) of cheese needed was the weight of an average family car.

MILK SQUIRTER

An Indian teenager has become a national celebrity for his ability to suck milk up through his nose and squirt it out of his eyes for distances of up to 12 ft (3.7 m). Praveen Kumar Sehrawat, a 16-year-old wrestler from the Delhi region, can also eat 170 chilies in just over five minutes and hammer a nail into his nose without suffering discomfort.

FAST FEATS

David Gonzales performed an astonishing 21 different strongman acts in a single afternoon in Fort Meyers, Florida, in November 2006. Ten of these were completed in less than a minute, including tearing a 1,000-page telephone book in half, bending a steel bar 4 in (10 cm) thick over his head, and standing on his head while holding himself steady with hands resting on broken glass.

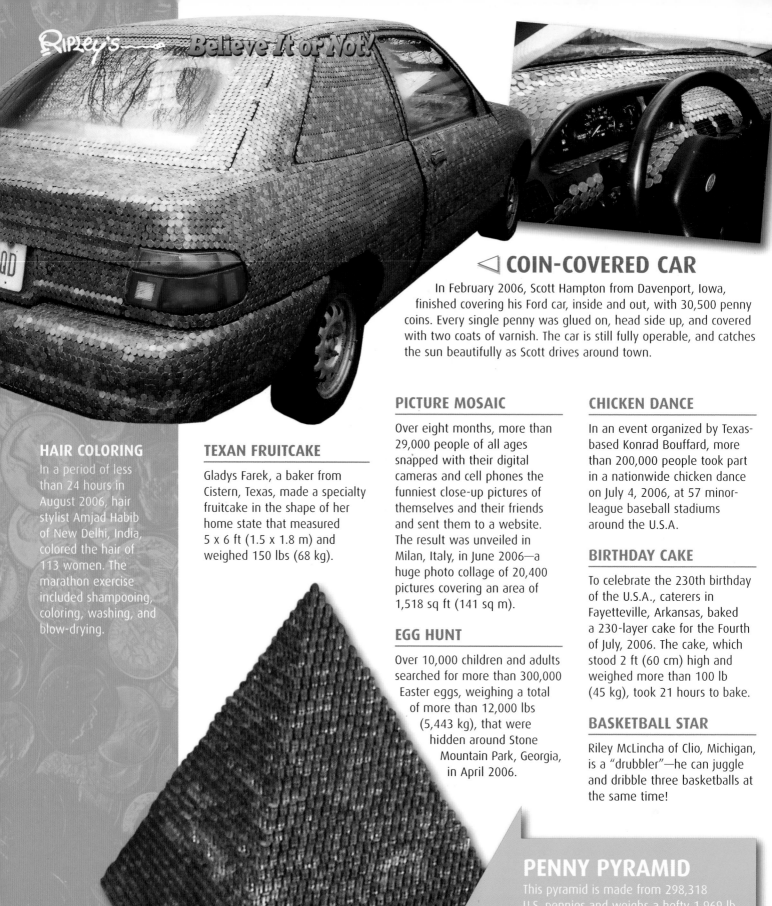

◁ COIN-COVERED CAR

In February 2006, Scott Hampton from Davenport, Iowa, finished covering his Ford car, inside and out, with 30,500 penny coins. Every single penny was glued on, head side up, and covered with two coats of varnish. The car is still fully operable, and catches the sun beautifully as Scott drives around town.

HAIR COLORING

In a period of less than 24 hours in August 2006, hair stylist Amjad Habib of New Delhi, India, colored the hair of 113 women. The marathon exercise included shampooing, coloring, washing, and blow-drying.

TEXAN FRUITCAKE

Gladys Farek, a baker from Cistern, Texas, made a specialty fruitcake in the shape of her home state that measured 5 x 6 ft (1.5 x 1.8 m) and weighed 150 lbs (68 kg).

PICTURE MOSAIC

Over eight months, more than 29,000 people of all ages snapped with their digital cameras and cell phones the funniest close-up pictures of themselves and their friends and sent them to a website. The result was unveiled in Milan, Italy, in June 2006—a huge photo collage of 20,400 pictures covering an area of 1,518 sq ft (141 sq m).

EGG HUNT

Over 10,000 children and adults searched for more than 300,000 Easter eggs, weighing a total of more than 12,000 lbs (5,443 kg), that were hidden around Stone Mountain Park, Georgia, in April 2006.

CHICKEN DANCE

In an event organized by Texas-based Konrad Bouffard, more than 200,000 people took part in a nationwide chicken dance on July 4, 2006, at 57 minor-league baseball stadiums around the U.S.A.

BIRTHDAY CAKE

To celebrate the 230th birthday of the U.S.A., caterers in Fayetteville, Arkansas, baked a 230-layer cake for the Fourth of July, 2006. The cake, which stood 2 ft (60 cm) high and weighed more than 100 lb (45 kg), took 21 hours to bake.

BASKETBALL STAR

Riley McLincha of Clio, Michigan, is a "drubbler"—he can juggle and dribble three basketballs at the same time!

PENNY PYRAMID

This pyramid is made from 298,318 U.S. pennies and weighs a hefty 1,969 lb (893 kg). Its creator, Marcelo Bezos from Miramar, Florida, has been building the pyramid since 1971, and he plans to continue adding to it until he reaches one million pennies. Each penny is placed individually, and Marcelo uses no adhesives of any kind.

Twists & Turns

Often training from as young as two years old, contortionists bend and twist their bodies into dramatic and unnatural-looking shapes, and, unsurprisingly, spend many years perfecting the art. Medical examinations of contortionists' spines have revealed that it is probably both genes and intensive training that allow them to get into such extreme shapes.

COLLECTIONS

Ripley's Believe It or Not!®

SURF'S UP!

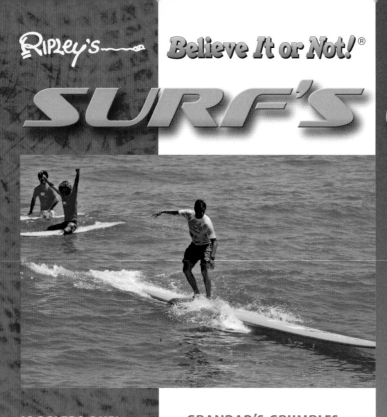

Brazilian surfing legend Rico de Souza rode a surfboard that measured an amazing 26 ft 5 in (8.05 m) in length at Macumba beach in Rio de Janeiro, Brazil, in November 2006. It had taken two months to develop a board strong enough to withstand the waves, and the result needed five people to lift it. De Souza managed to paddle the huge board into the sea and to stand up on it, alone, on the crest of a wave, for 11 seconds.

JOGGLERS DUEL

The 2006 Boston Marathon provided a unique spectacle: the first time two jogglers—runners who juggle—had competed head-to-head in a marathon. The combatants were Zach Warren, from West Virginia, an expert juggler who can juggle blindfold and while riding a unicycle, and Michal Kapral, who once ran the marathon in his home city of Toronto, Canada, in 2 hours 49 minutes— while pushing his baby daughter Annika in a stroller. In Boston, Kapral juggled three bean-filled balls and Warren juggled three beanbags, never taking more than two steps without juggling. Warren (911th overall) emerged the winner of their personal duel in a time of just under three hours, with Kapral 8 minutes behind in 1,761st place.

GRANDAD'S GRUMBLES

An unlikely Internet hero emerged in 2006—a 79-year-old British grandfather, Peter Oakley. Peter hit the top of the most subscribed list on a popular free video sharing website with his ramblings and grumbles about the modern world. Equipped with headphones and a mike, he posted a series of videocasts, attracting some 30,000 subscribers. He also received more than 4,500 e-mails from fans in Japan, U.S.A., Australia, Germany, and Ireland.

CLOG DANCE

Nearly 500 teenagers from 26 countries donned oversized wooden clogs to perform a modern ballet version of a traditional Dutch clog dance in The Hague in July 2006. The dancers learned the steps in their own countries, which included Canada, Jamaica, Israel, and Finland, before traveling to the Netherlands for the performance.

WORD PERFECT

Mahaveer Jain of Lucknow, India, has memorized the entire *Oxford Advanced Learner's Dictionary*, which includes 80,000 entries in all!

GIANT CROQUETTE

Cooks in Assabu, Japan, made a croquette nearly 7 ft (2.1 m) in diameter. It contained 397 lb (180 kg) of potatoes mixed with meat and onions and, at 705 lb (320 kg), was so heavy that a crane had to lower it into a vat containing 67 gal (252 l) of salad oil. The giant croquette was then cut into 1,300 pieces for visitors to taste.

HAPPY SHOPPER

In 2005, Edd China from Maidenhead, Berkshire, England, built a motorized shopping cart that can hit speeds of 60 mph (97 km/h). China, who has previously built a motorized sofa, shed, and four-poster bed, spent six months designing the cart, which is over 11 ft (3.3 m) tall, nearly 10 ft (3 m) long and 6 ft (2 m) wide. It is powered by a 600cc motorbike engine hidden in a huge shopping bag, while the driver sits in an oversized child seat.

PRIZE PEACH

Paul Friday of Coloma, Michigan, has grown a peach that weighs an incredible 30½ oz (864 g).

LIGHT DISPLAY

October 2005 saw 24,581 jack-o-lanterns lit up on Boston Common, Massachusetts, in a mass gathering of more than 45,000 people.

EXTREME CROQUET

Bob Warseck of West Hartford, Connecticut, enjoys a game of croquet—but not on a conventional lawn. Warseck is a pioneer of the sport of extreme croquet, which is played through woods, over rocks, up and down hills, and across streams. He and his fellow players have had to design special heavy-duty mallets to cope with the rough terrain.

PAPER FOLDERS

In 2006, a total of 545 nimble-fingered staff and students from the National University of Singapore folded 9,300 origami paper cranes in just one hour.

PREGNANT ROBOT

At Kaiser Permanente Hospital in Vallejo, California, doctors teach students by using a full-size "pregnant" robot patient, Noelle, to simulate giving birth!

CORNY PROPOSAL

When Brian Rueckl proposed to Stacy Martin in the summer of 2006, he did it in style—in the form of a message measuring 4,000 sq ft (372 sq m) tilled in his boss's cornfield near Luxemburg, Wisconsin. The message read "Stacy will you marry me?" and included two intersecting hearts. The unusual proposal required a year of planning and 40 hours of work. Naturally, Stacy accepted.

FISH FEAST

An Irish pub in Boston, Massachusetts, served a portion of fish and chips weighing a colossal 77 lbs (35 kg)—34 lbs (15 kg) for the cod fillet and 43 lbs (20 kg) for the fries.

LONG LUNCH

For one weekend a year, husband-and-wife chefs Doug and Helen Turpin find themselves preparing a larger Sunday lunch than usual. They are responsible for "The Long Lunch," an annual barbecue at Warkworth, Ontario, Canada, that stretches on tables 500 ft (152 m) down the village's main street and draws as many as 1,000 people from as far afield as Europe. The Long Lunch is based on a similar event offered by its twin town of Warkworth, New Zealand.

BALLOON HATS

At Hillsboro, Oregon, in 2006, 20 volunteers used air pumps to blow up 7,000 balloons—so that they could be used as hats! Over 1,800 people then gathered for a group photo in the Civic Center Plaza, wearing the inflatable headgear.

NINE-HOUR RAP

In 2006, rapper Supernatural performed a freestyle rap in San Bernardino, California, that went on for an incredible 9 hours 10 minutes! Afterward, he said that the hardest parts were keeping his breath and pacing himself.

A SKIP AND A JUMP

Kyle Nolte from Fort Smith, Arkansas, is a pogo stick fanatic. Not only can he jump rope while hopping up and down on his pogo stick, but he can also play baseball and hula hoop while pogoing.

PANCAKE FLIP

Nobody tosses a pancake quite like Dean Gould of Felixstowe, Suffolk, England. For Gould, renowned for his dexterity at flipping beer mats, can also toss a pancake 424 times in two minutes. He practiced his new skill with a plate and a Whoopee cushion!

HOOP HEROINE

Betty Shurin of Aspen, Colorado, ran a 6-mi (10-km) race at Boulder in 2005 in 1 hour 43 minutes 11 seconds—while hula hooping. In order to make sure the hoop was never accidentally knocked down, Shurin, who has been hula hooping since 1998, surrounded herself with a "bubble" of friends throughout the race. "I communicated with the bubble and it communicated with me," said Shurin. "For every water station, they would circle around me and hold hands. I had about three inches of mistake room."

BRUSH OFF

As part of a special challenge, at exactly 1:45 p.m. on August 7, 2006, some 32,000 people—both young and old—across New Zealand brushed their teeth simultaneously.

TEAM EFFORT

Thirty students from the Ishii Higashi Elementary School in Japan ran a 31-legged race over 164 ft (50 m) in a time of 8.8 seconds in October 2005.

CAR CRUSH

Twenty-one Malaysian students, all of whom were over the age of 18, somehow managed to cram themselves into a Mini Cooper in June 2006. And what's more they had to do it twice after the TV crew sent to cover the event turned up late!

ROCKET MAN

Thousands of people flocked to the 2006 U.K. Fireworks Championships in Plymouth, Devon, to see 55,000 rockets launched simultaneously. The idea was the brainchild of Roy Lowry who, by using 15 specially constructed frames that were laced with a pyrotechnic fuse and ignited electrically, managed to launch all the rockets in the space of five seconds.

CHOCOLATE ▷ SCULPTURE

The Portuguese village of Obidos, lying 50 mi (80 km) north of the capital Lisbon, fulfilled a chocoholic's dream in November 2006 when it played host to the Chocolate Festival. The festival included an exhibition of chocolate sculpture, which featured this chocolate car and chocolate Marilyn Monroe.

BALLOON MURAL

A mural of the Chicago skyline, 58 x 86 ft (18 x 26 m), made from 70,000 balloons was once displayed in Rosemont, Illinois.

SKIMMING CHAMPION

Dougie Isaacs of Scotland was crowned World Stone Skimming Champion in 2005 at a disused quarry in Argyll. Each of the 220 competitors was allowed five skims using special slate stones. The stone had to bounce on the water surface at least three times and was then judged on the distance it traveled before sinking. Isaacs hit the flooded quarry's back wall, recording a distance of 207 ft (63 m).

CAR HURDLER

This amazing montage of images shows Jeff Clay of Rossville, Georgia, performing the astonishing feat of hurdling lengthwise over a car. Clay, who hurdles in the correct style of track athletes, also hurdles cars widthwise, and once jumped 101 different cars that were lined up inside a track stadium in 38 minutes flat.

RIVER BATTLE

Snowmobiles are primarily designed for traveling on land in the depths of winter, but in 2006, Greg Nielsen covered over 59 mi (95 km) on one—on water in summer. Tackling the Wapiti River, Alberta, Canada, he faced a constant battle to keep water out of the machine. He said: "I just talked nicely to the sled the whole way and hoped the engine held together."

BARE DEVIL

A Nepali high-altitude guide posed on the summit of Mount Everest in 2006—in the nude! After reaching the top of the world's highest mountain, Lakpa Tharke took off his clothes on the icy peak where the temperature was –40°F (–40°C). Lapka, who climbed the mountain as part of a 14-member expedition led by American Luis Benitez, stayed in the buff for three minutes so that his companions could photograph him.

GAS SAVER

A team of engineering students from the University of British Columbia built a vehicle so efficient it could travel from Vancouver to Halifax—the entire breadth of Canada—on just a gallon of gasoline. In tests, it achieved an amazing 3,145 mi (5,060 km) to the U.S. gallon, the only possible drawback being that the futuristic, single-occupancy vehicle requires the driver to lie down while navigating it.

SCROLL DOWN

Jack Kerouac wrote the classic novel *On The Road* in 20 days, typing it onto a single 119-ft (36-m) scroll!

STILT DANCERS

Thirty-four members of the Lieder Youth Theatre Company line-danced on stilts for 6 minutes 15 seconds at Goulburn, New South Wales, Australia, in January 2006.

GENETIC MUSIC

In 2003, composer Richard Krull and researchers Aurora Sanchez Sousa and Fernando Baquero of Ramon y Cajal Hospital in Madrid, Spain, turned DNA sequences into music and recorded a CD.

BURGER QUEST

Retired teacher Bill Bunyan of Dodge City, Kansas, set off in June 2000 with the intention of eating a hamburger in all 105 counties in the state. He completed his journey in Sterling in August 2003 on his 65th birthday in the presence of friends who had been sent hamburger-shaped invitations by his wife Susan.

LETTER WRITER

Whenever he has something to say, Jacob Sahayam of Trivandrum, India, writes a letter to a newspaper. In 2005, he had no fewer than 523 letters published by the editors of various newspapers and magazines, easily beating his previous year's total of 340.

Bottled Cards

Vancouver master magician Jamie Grant has told nobody how he managed to insert an unopened pack of playing cards into this glass bottle.

BRIGHT IDEA

An artist who once tried to leave a tap running for 12 months to highlight water wastage and pushed a peanut across London with his nose to highlight student debt came up with a new project in 2006—to leave 100 lightbulbs on for a year. Mark McGowan arranged for the lights—at different locations across London and southeast England—to be left on until August 2007 in the hope of making people aware of the waste of electricity.

HOCKEY TAPE

In June 2006, 12-year-old Ryan Funk of Langley, British Columbia, Canada, assembled a ball out of ice hockey tape that weighed an incredible 1,862 lb (845 kg). The tape had been donated by 19 ice rinks across Canada.

SKATE CHAIN

Some 280 Singaporeans strapped on their wheels, clutched the waist of the person in front, and formed an in-line skating chain that snaked through the streets of Singapore City in August 2006.

Ripley's Believe It or Not!

QUICK SHAVE

In April 2006, a team of five hairdressers shaved 662 heads in just four hours at Sudbury, Ontario, Canada.

BIG BOWL

In 2004, Australian chefs cooked a 7.5-ton bowl of risotto—a rice dish—that was so big it took paddles the size of oars to stir it!

BUSY BUBBLE

Canadian bubble artist Fan Yang linked 15 pairs of people in a "bubble cage" at the Discovery Science Center in Santa Ana, California, in April 2006. The following month he encapsulated 22 people inside a single soap bubble in Madrid, Spain.

THREE-LEGGED RACE

Ben Scott and Jo Gittens from the Isle of Man competed in the London Marathon three-legged and dressed as fairies! Their legs tied together with a scarf, they finished in an impressive 5 hours 45 minutes.

DRUM BEAT

Col Hatchman, drummer with Sydney, Australia, rock band Dirty Skanks, drums so loudly it is the equivalent of listening to a jet plane taking off 100 ft (30 m) away! In 2006, he recorded a massive 137 decibels, compared to the 85 decibels of busy city center traffic.

TUNNEL VISION

Germany's Christian Adams specializes in cycling backward while playing the violin. Adams, who has been playing the instrument since 1970, once cycled over 37 mi (60 km) backward through a Swiss highway tunnel while playing Bach on his violin.

150-SLICE PIZZA

Mama Lena's Pizza House in McKees Rocks, Pennsylvania, produces a commercially available 53½-in (136-cm) pizza that offers 150 slices, for $99.99. It contains 20 lb (9 kg) of dough, 15 lb (6.8 kg) of cheese, and 1 gal (4 l) of sauce.

CREAM DRESS

Ukrainian baker Valentyn Shtefano created an edible wedding dress for his bride. Made from 1,500 cream puffs, the dress weighed 20 lb (9 kg) and took him two months to complete.

IN DEPTH
THE GREAT ESCAPE

World-renowned escape artist David Straitjacket, from Manchester, England, can release himself from straitjackets, handcuffs, and ropes within minutes. Dubbed the "Modern Houdini," he claims the old master had it easy!

How did you discover your talent for escaping?

"When I was about seven, me and my cousins played a game tying each other to chairs. I was by far the best at getting free!"

When did you decide to pursue it?

"When I was 13 I was a Sea Cadet and we spent a week with the older boys who were going into the Navy. Two 18-year-olds were bullying us, making us wash their dishes! I refused, so they tied me to the sink and left me there. Two minutes later I caught up with them and handed them the rope. They left me alone after that... that was probably when I thought: 'I am going to do this for a job!'"

When did you get your first straitjacket?

"About 10 years ago. I was a poor street performer and bought it cheap. It tore in half the first time I used it. I spent the next week rebuilding it to make it strong enough for me."

Is your body "different" from everyone else's?

"I have very nimble fingers which are good for picking locks, but I'm not double-jointed and can't dislocate my joints."

What is the most dangerous escape you have attempted?

"I was in China on a huge lake. It was murky and deep. The Chinese police took me out on a boat tied up with three pairs of handcuffs and about 10 kg of chain with two padlocks. I jumped off, hit the bottom about four meters down, and couldn't see more than six inches. I had no safety divers. It was touch and go."

So do you have to practice?

"Yes! I have a strong working knowledge of locks and cuffs. I fiddle with handcuffs while I'm sitting watching the TV. On top of that, you have to have a natural talent—and a few personal trade secrets!"

Do you do any mental training—and is it true you don't like enclosed spaces?

"I'm actually really quite claustrophobic! I train myself to relax. If you panic, you fail. Underwater, you've got three minutes to escape, but if you panic, you run out of oxygen in just one minute."

How do you cope with injuries?

"I carry on. I did a televised escape called 'Barbed Wire' five days after I'd had surgery on my shoulder. I was bruised all over my chest and arm—the make-up department had a field day. I had barbed wire round my neck, attached to a chain between my legs, which led to more barbed wire round my wrists. I was padlocked, handcuffed, and hung upside down by my feet."

Are you "the modern Houdini?"

"I understand people say that as a compliment—but I'm just me. He used to do the straitjacket escape in about 80 or 90 minutes—he'd disappear behind a curtain for that long while the orchestra played, then appear again. If I'm still going at 90 seconds, people get bored! These days we have much shorter attention spans... and better locks."

What will you try next?

"I'm preparing for some big high-risk stunts. One involves the Burj al-Arab building in Dubai, and me training in free-fall parachuting, to give you a clue!"

HONEY TRAP

Denzil St. Clair of Spencer, Ohio, allowed himself to be covered from head to toe in more than half a million honey bees in June 2006. He wore a mask that covered his nose and mouth, goggles to protect his eyes, and stuck cotton in his ears, but he was still stung up to 30 times. He said afterward: "It was like being blind, covered with wet towels, and very hot."

YOUNG UNICYCLIST

Whereas other youngsters are into skateboards, 19-year-old Jonny Peacock of Shalimar, Florida, is a budding extreme unicyclist. He can walk on his wheel and twist it 360 degrees, jump off picnic tables on a unicycle, and zigzag between wooden posts. He owns five different unicycles, including one called the "giraffe" with an elongated seat and another called the "impossible wheel" that has no seat at all.

⚠ EYE BLOWER

In 2005, Yu Hongqua from China blew out candles with his eyes using a specially crafted pair of glasses with air tubes attached.

HUGE UMBRELLA

In October 2005, Sun City Umbrella Industries of Jin Jiang city, China, made an umbrella that was 31½ ft (9.6 m) tall and over 53 ft (16 m) in diameter.

BODY PAINTING

At Sherman, New York, in July 2006, body artists Scott Fray and Madelyn Greco of Reidsville, North Carolina, sponged 337 people in head-to-toe non-toxic washable paint. The volunteers then laid down in a colorful pattern to be photographed from a passing helicopter.

APPLE PICKER

George Adrian of Indianapolis, Indiana, once picked 30,000 apples in one eight-hour day—that's about 1,000 lb (454 kg) every hour!

NOODLE TREE

Workers at a hotel in Bangkok, Thailand, spent 16 hours creating a Christmas tree 17 ft 4 in (5.3 m) tall made entirely from noodles and decorated with colored sugar.

LIZARD BOY

Mukesh Thakore, a 29-year-old Indian man, has eaten more than 25,000 lizards over the past 20 years! He first became addicted to eating the reptiles as a five-year-old when, spotting a lizard in the wild, he popped it in his mouth out of curiosity. Now Thakore, known locally as the Lizard Boy, devours up to 25 live lizards every day for breakfast, lunch, and dinner.

HARPISTS' HUDDLE

A total of 45 harpists (ranging in age from 5 to 55) gathered in the town of Harlech's 13th-century castle in north Wales, to play a concert in 2006. It was the first time so many harpists had played simultaneously in a Welsh castle.

⚠ TONGUE BURNER

An Indian performer touches his tongue with fire, apparently without damage, in New Delhi in 2006.

TOUGH GUY

Running through flames, this participant takes part in the 2006 Tough Guy competition held in England. The contest is designed to test physical and mental endurance on an assault course and an 8-mi (13-km) country run. In 2006, a total of 4,515 competitors entered but only 3,235 are recorded to have finished, in times that varied from 1 hour 17 minutes to 4 hours.

Index

A

Aberg, David (Swe) 16
Acton, Pat (U.S.A.) 12
Adams, Christian (Ger) 30
Adrian, George (U.S.A.) 32
air guitar contest 12
Amritanandamayi, Mata (Ind) 8
animals, balloon 13
apples, speed picking 32

B

babies, crawling marathon 19
balloons
    animals made from 13
    blowing up with ears and
        eyes 8–9, 9
    as hats 27
    inflating multiple 16
    mural of Chicago 28
balls
    giant rubber-band ball 14,
        14–15
    hockey-tape ball 29
    juggling and dribbling
        basketballs simultaneously
        24
    juggling shot balls 13, 13
    tinfoil ball 8
Baquero, Fernando (Spa) 29
barbecue, Long Lunch 27
bees, man covered in 32
bells, bicycle bell music 9
Benitez, Luis (U.S.A.) 29
Bezos, Marcelo (U.S.A.) 24, 24
bicycles
    bicycle bell music 9
    playing violin while cycling
        backwards 30
Bilbrey, Braxton (U.S.A.) 8
Billmeier, Craig (U.S.A.) 12
birds, penguins air-lifted to
    safety 19
boats, water-skiing behind cruise
    liner 19
bottle, playing-cards in 29, 29
Bouffard, Konrad (U.S.A.) 24
bowling
    in every county in Kansas 19
    simultaneous games 12, 12
bras, chain of 19
Brasil, Ary (Bra) 8
Breen, Tom (U.S.A.) 9, 9
Bright, Ivan (U.S.A.) 19
"bubble cage," people in 30
buffet, huge selection 8
buildings, newspaper models 10,
    10
Bunyan, Bill (U.S.A.) 29
Burrows, Terry (U.K.) 16

C

cakes
    giant Fourth of July cake 24
    Texas-shaped fruitcake 24
candles, blowing out with eyes
    32, 32
cars
    all-terrain vehicle parade 16
    chocolate sculpture of 28, 28
    covered in coins 24, 24
    extremely economical 29
    hurdling over 28, 28–29
    large number of people in 28
    pulling with eyelids 18, 18
    pulling with hair 8, 8
    radio plays engine sounds 10
cartoons, drawing
        simultaneously with hands
        and feet 9, 9
cartwheels, simultaneous 22
Cassidy, John (U.S.A.) 16
cathedrals, extreme cellists on
    12
Chestnut, Joey (U.S.A.) 10
Chicago, balloon mural of 28
chicken, speed eating 10
chicken dance, nationwide 24
children
    drum player 10, 10
    long-distance swimmer 8
China, Edd (U.K.) 27
chocolate, sculpture 28, 28
Christmas tree, made of
    noodles 32
Christou, Al (Can) 22
cigarette wrappers, tinfoil ball 8
Clarke, Stephen (U.S.A.) 8
Clay, Jeff (U.S.A.) 28, 28–29
clog dance 26
clothes
    edible wedding dress 30, 30
    enormous sari 10
cobras, kissing 17, 17
coins
    car covered in 24
    pyramid of 24, 24
collage, huge photo 24
combine harvesters, speed
    harvest 8
contortionists 25, 25
Cook, Ben (U.S.A.) 16
cornfield, marriage proposal in
    27
crawling marathon, for babies
    19
Crazy Richard (U.S.A.) 13
croquet, extreme 27
croquette, giant 27
cruise liner, water-skiing behind
    19

D

dancing
    clog dance 26
    line-dancing on stilts 29
    nationwide chicken dance 24
Dawson, Jeremy (U.K.) 12
de Souza, Rico (Bra) 26, 26
Deeble, Carol (U.S.A.) 12
Di Fater, Michael "Mickey"
    (U.S.A.) 19
dictionary, memorizing 26
DNA sequences turned into
    music 29
dogs
    on charity motorcycle run 9
    skydiving 22
    surfing 10
drawings
    giant teapot 12
    with hands and feet
        simultaneously 9, 9
drinking straws, long chain of 18
drums
    child player 10, 10
    noisy 30

E

ears, blowing up balloons with
    8–9, 9
Easter egg hunt 24
electricity, wasting 29
escapology
    David Straitjacket 31, 31
    from box of cement 6, 6–7
Everest, Mount, nude on summit
    29
extreme sports, croquet 27
eyelids, pulling car with 18, 18
eyes
    blowing candles out with 32,
        32
    blowing up balloons with 8–9,
        9
    squirting milk out of 22

F

Farek, Gladys (U.S.A.) 24
fire
    running through 33, 33
    touching with tongue 32, 32
fireworks, mass rocket launch
    28
fish and chips, giant portion 27
flag, human depiction of 19
food
    eating insects 10
    eating lizards 32
    edible wedding dress 30, 30
    giant bowl of risotto 30
    giant croquette 27
    giant Fourth of July cake 24
    giant portion of fish and chips
        27
    huge selection at buffet 8
    Long Lunch 27
    mass pizza delivery 22
    speed eating 10
    Texas-shaped fruitcake 24

footprints, long chain of paper
    18
Fray, Scott (U.S.A.) 32
Friday, Paul (U.S.A.) 27
Fuji, Mount, climbing on pogo
    stick 9
Funk, Ryan (Can) 29
Furman, Ashrita (U.S.A.) 9

G

Gagnon, Nicole-Anne (Can) 10
gasoline, extremely economical
    car 29
Gion, Dirk (Ger) 19
Gittens, Jo (U.K.) 30
golf, playing in space 9
Gonzales, David (U.S.A.) 23, 23
Gould, Dean (U.K.) 28
Grant, Jamie (Can) 29, 29
Greco, Madelyn (U.S.A.) 32
guitars
    air guitar contest 12
    mass Jimi Hendrix play-in 9
    playing for long time 16
Gunnarson, Dean (Can) 6, 6–7

H

Habib, Amjad (Ind) 24
hair
    mass shaving event 30
    multiple coloring 24
    pulling car with 8, 8
    speed cutting 22
hamburgers, eating in every
    state of Kansas 29
Hamid, Shahimi Abdul (Mal) 17,
    17
Hampton, Scott 24, 24
harps, multiple players 32
harvest, speedy 8
Hatchman, Col (Aus) 30
hats, balloons as 27
Hendrix, Jimi (U.S.A.) 9
hockey-tape ball 29
hot dogs, long-time salesman 19
Houdini, Harry (U.S.A.) 6, 31
Huet, Patrick (Fra) 9
hula hoops
    running race 28
    spinning multiple 10
Hunt, Doug (Can) 16
hurdling over car 28, 28–29

I

Indian Ocean, crossing on
    sailboard 20–21, 20–21
insects, eating 10
Internet, grumbling grandad 26
Isaacs, Dougie (U.K.) 28
Ishii Higashi Elementary School
    (Jap) 28

J

jack-o-lanterns, mass display 27
Jain, Mahaveer (Ind) 26

Jollymore, Stanley (Can) 8
journalists, underwater press conference 22
juggling
    joggler marathon 26
    juggling and dribbling basketballs simultaneously 24
    shot balls 13, *13*

K

Kapral, Michael (U.S.A.) 26
Kärger, Jörg (Ger) 9
Kasibhatia, Nishant (Ind) 22
kazoo parade 19
Keegan, Kevin (U.K.) 22
Kerouac, Jack (U.S.A.) 29
kick line, very long 18
kissing cobras 17, *17*
Krull, Richard (Spa) 29

L

Lakpa Tharke (Nep) 29
Le Gouvello, Raphaela (Fra) 20–21, *20–21*
lecture, extremely long 12
letters, published in newspapers 29
lights, leaving on for a year 29
line-dancing, on stilts 29
lizards, eating 32
Lomeli, Lori Lynn (U.S.A.) 10
Lowry, Roy (U.K.) 28

M

McGowan, Mark (U.K.) 29
McLincha, Riley (U.S.A.) 24
Mama Lena's Pizza House (U.S.A.) 30
marriage proposal, in cornfield 27
Martin, Stacy (U.S.A.) 27
Marx, Groucho (U.S.A.) 8
matchstick models 12
memory
    memorizing dictionary 26
    memorizing numbers 22
Mikulich, Nate (U.S.A.) 13
milk
    speed drinking 10
    squirting out of eyes 22
Milton, Steve (U.S.A.) 14, *14–15*
Mitchell, Trevor (U.K.) 22
Monroe, Marilyn (U.S.A.), chocolate sculpture of 28, *28*
Moore, Robert (U.S.A.) 12, *12*
motorcycles
    dogs on charity run 9
    motorized shopping cart 27
Mottashed, Brad (Can) 18
mountains
    Mount Everest, nude on summit 29

Mount Fuji, climbing on pogo stick 9
mouth, huge spoon in 19, *19*
murals
    huge 19
    made of balloons 28
Murphy, Ryan (U.S.A.) 18
music, DNA sequences turned into 29
musical instruments
    bicycle bells 9
    child drum player 10, *10*
    extreme cellists 12
    kazoo parade 19
    mass Jimi Hendrix play-in 9
    multiple harp players 32
    playing guitar for long time 16
    playing violin on unicycle 16
    playing violin while cycling backwards 30

N

nail polish, painting with 22, *22*
names, gathering of Joneses 22
newspapers
    mass letter-writer 29
    models made from 10, *10*
Nielsen, Greg (Can) 29
Nolte, Kyle (U.S.A.) 27, *27*
noodles, Christmas tree made of 32
novel, typed on scroll 29
nude, on summit of Mount Everest 29
numbers, memorizing 22

O

Oakley, Peter (U.K.) 26
origami, mass folding 27

P

paintings
    body painting 32
    giant 16
    huge mural 19
    with nail polish 22, *22*
pancakes, speed tossing 28
Papa John's (U.S.A.) 22
paper
    long chain of footprints 18
    mass origami folding 27
park, car parking space turned into temporary 10
Pavone, Julian (U.S.A.) 10, *10*
peach, giant 27
Peacock, Jonny (U.S.A.) 32
penguins, air-lifted to safety 19
photos, huge collage 24
pillow fight, giant 16
pizzas
    giant 30
    mass delivery 22
playing cards, in bottle 29, *29*

Plugge, Jay and Jason (U.S.A.) 10
poem, extremely long 9
pogo sticks 27, *27*
    climbing Mount Fuji on 9
Polo, Eddie (U.S.A.) 8, *8*
"pregnant" robot 27
Presley, Elvis, impersonators 19
press conference, underwater 22
pumpkin, speed carving 8
pyramid, of coins 24, *24*

R

radio, plays engine sounds 10
Ramesh, Anniah (Ind) 12
rap, very long 27
Rebar (U.S.A.) 10
Rees, James (U.K.) 12
Revere, Paul (U.S.A.) 9
risotto, giant bowl of 30
Robin Hood 12
robot, "pregnant" teaching aid 27
rockets, mass launch 28
roller coaster, wedding on 12
Roskopf, Milan (Slo) 13, *13*
Rowling, J.K. (U.K.) 12
rubber-band ball, giant 14, *14–15*
Rueckl, Brian (U.S.A.) 27
running
    backwards 8
    joggler marathon 26
    three-legged races 28, 30
Russell, Roderick (U.S.A.) 11, *11*

S

Sahayam, Jacob (Ind) 29
sailboard, solo crossing of Indian Ocean 20–21, *20–21*
St. Clair, Denzil (U.S.A.) 32
Sanchez Sousa, Aurora (Spa) 29
sari, enormous 10
Sarver, Jef (U.S.A.) 16
Schwickrath, Pete (U.S.A.) 16, *16*
Scott, Ben (U.K.) 30
Scott, Mary (U.S.A.) 22, *22*
sculpture
    chocolate 28, *28*
    tin foil 16, *16*
Sehrawat, Praveen Kumar (Ind) 22
shaving, mass event 30
sheep, riding rodeo-style 18
shopping cart, motorized 27
Shtefano, Valentyn 30, *30*
Shurin, Betty (U.S.A.) 28
skating chain 29
skydiving dog 22

smoothie, enormous 12
snakes, kissing cobras 17, *17*
snowballs, mass fight 18
snowmobiles, on water 29
Soloff, Edward (U.S.A.) 12, *12*
spelling, backwards 22
spoons
    huge spoon in mouth 19, *19*
    multiple players 8
Srivathsav, Raghav (Ind) 22
stilts
    line-dancing on 29
    tall stilts 16
stone-skimming contest 28
Straitjacket, David (U.K.) 31, *31*
strongman stunts 23, *23*
Supernatural (U.S.A.) 27
surfboard, extremely long 26, *26*
surfing, dogs 10
swimming, child swims from Alcatraz to San Francisco 8
swords, swallowing 11, *11*
Sydney Opera House (Aus), Perspex model of 13

T

teeth, simultaneous brushing 28
texting, speed 16
Thakore, Mukesh (Ind) 32
three-legged races 28, 30
thumbs, speed texting 16
tin foil
    ball of 8
    sculpture 16, *16*
tongue, touching fire with 32, *32*
towel, giant beach 16
trees, noodle Christmas tree 32
Tretick, Drew (U.S.A.) 16
truck, drinking from 19
Turpin, Doug and Helen (Can) 27
Tuttle, Don (U.S.A.) 12
Tyurin, Mikhail (Rus) 9

U

umbrella, giant 32
underwater press conference 22
unicycles 32
    playing violin on 16

V

vending machine, child in 12, *12*
Venkov, Evgueni (Can) 18
violins
    playing on unicycle 16
    playing while cycling backward 30

W

Wallace, Clare (U.K.) 12
Warren, Zach (U.S.A.) 26
Warseck, Bob (U.S.A.) 27
water-skiing, behind cruise liner
    19
watermelons, giant 19
weddings
    edible dress 30, *30*
    on roller coaster 12
weights
    juggling shot balls 13, *13*
    pulling car with eyelids 18, *18*
    pulling car with hair 8, *8*
Wereski, Don (U.S.A.) 9
windows, speedy cleaning 16
words
    memorizing dictionary 26
    spelling backwards 22
Woydziak, Larry (U.S.A.) 19

Y

Yang, Fan (Can) 30
Yang Guanghe (Chn) 18, *18*

Z

Zhang Dong (Chn) 19, *19*
Zhang Yingmin (Chn) *8–9*, 9
Zhu Zhonge (Chn) 10, *10*

ACKNOWLEDGMENTS

COVER (t/l) Courtesy of David Straitjacket, (t/r) Spectrum Multi-Media Ltd. George Douklias—Winnipeg www.AlwaysEscaping.com; 4 Roderick Russell/CNY Medical Center; 6 (t, b) Spectrum Multi-Media Ltd. Kent Hart—Hart Images www.AlwaysEscaping.com; 7 (t/r) Spectrum Multi-Media Ltd. George Douklias—Winnipeg www.AlwaysEscaping.com, (t/l) Spectrum Multi-Media Ltd. Kent Hart—Hart Images www.AlwaysEscaping.com, (c, b) Spectrum Multi-Media Ltd. George Douklias—Winnipeg www.AlwaysEscaping.com; 8–9 (dp) Duan Renhu/Phototex/Camera Press London; 8 (fc) Karin Lau/Fotolia.com; 10 (t) Newscom, (b) Feature China/Barcroft Media; 11 Roderick Russell/CNY Medical Center; 12 (b) PA Photos; 13 Reuters/Alexandra Beier; 14–15 Reuters/Frank Polich; 14 (fc) Johanna Goodyear/Fotolia.com; 16 Pete Schwickrath/Ripley Entertainment Inc.; 18 Camera Press/Wu Dongjun/Phototex; 19 Reuters/Sean Yong; 20–21 (dp) Richard Bouhet/AFP/Getty Images; 20 (b) Tony Ashby/AFP/Getty Images; 21 (t) Tony Ashby/AFP/Getty Images; 22 (fc) Mary Scott/Ripley Entertainment Inc., (t/l) Mehmet Dilsiz/Fotolia.com, (t/r) Mary Scott/Ripley Entertainment Inc.; 24 (t/l, t/r) Scott Hampton/Ripley Entertainment Inc., (b) Marcelo Bezos/Ripley Entertainment Inc.; 25 (t/r) Reuters/Alex Grimm, (t/l) Reuters/Daniel Aguilar, (c/r) PA Photos, (c/l) Reuters/Mohamed Azakir, (b) Reuters/China Photos; 26 Reuters/Sergio Moraes; 27 Kyle Nolte/Ripley Entertainment Inc.; 28–29 (b,dp) Jeff Clay/Ripley Enteimtent Inc.; 28 (t) Reuters/Jose Manuel Ribeiro; 29 (t) Jamie Grant/Ripley Entertainment Inc.; 30 PA Photos; 31 Courtesy of David Straitjacket; 32–33 (dp) Reuters/Darren Staples; 32 (t) Camera Press/Zhang Xiangyang/Phototex, (b) Reuters/Kamal Kishore

All other photos are from Corel, PhotoDisc, Digital Vision and Ripley's Entertainment Inc.